Eulogies
When
Violent Crime
Takes Our Beloved:

Writing Guidelines, Examples And Templates

With Tips For Grieving, Healing And Moving On

J Jordan

Notable+

Copyright & Disclaimer

EULOGIES WHEN VIOLENT CRIME TAKES OUR BELOVED:
WRITING GUIDELINES, EXAMPLES AND TEMPLATES

Eulogies When Violent Crime Takes Our Beloved: Writing Guidelines, Examples And Templates
Paperback: 103 Pages
Print Quality: Black ink and 55# (90 GSM) cream paper
ISBN-10: 1-960176-18-8
ISBN-13: 978-1-960176-18-9

Contents

Preface

Firstly, please accept my deepest condolences. Losing a loved one is an incredibly challenging experience, and I sincerely pray that you find the strength to endure during this time of immense pain and loss.

Honoring The Memory Of A Loved One Lost To Violent Crime

Losing a loved one is always a painful and devastating experience, but when their life is taken as a result of criminal acts, the pain can feel even more overwhelming. In times like these, finding a way to pay tribute to their memory becomes crucial. One powerful way to do so is by writing a fitting eulogy that captures the essence of who they were and the impact they had on the world. In this book/ebook we will explore the process of crafting a heartfelt eulogy for someone lost to criminal acts, and provide guidance and support during this time of difficulty.

The Purpose Of This Book

Within the pages of this book, we address the multitude of challenges that arise when writing a eulogy for someone who passed away due to violent crime. We provide heartfelt eulogy examples and a step-by-step guide to assist you in crafting and delivering a truly meaningful eulogy. In addition, we provide comprehensive answers to commonly asked questions that cover a wide range of topics, such as crafting and organizing the eulogy, handling cherished memories, navigating through grief, and facilitating the healing process.

Writing an empowering eulogy for a loved one lost to crime is not just about honoring the memory of our loved ones; it is also about demanding change and justice. By celebrating their lives, remembering their unique qualities, and addressing the broader issues that led to their loss, we can make a powerful impact both in healing our own hearts and in advocating for a more just and compassionate society.

This book has been meticulously crafted to equip you with the essential tools for navigating the process of writing and delivering a eulogy, all while managing the overwhelming emotions that come with such a difficult period. Our ultimate objective is not only to assist you in creating and delivering a eulogy that truly honors the departed, but also to empower you to navigate the stages of grief and ultimately find solace, healing, and the strength to move forward.

In Difficulty You Are Strengthened

When news of the passing of a loved one arrives, and you find yourself overwhelmed with emotions while simultaneously planning the funeral and holding the rest of the family together, writing a eulogy becomes an arduous task. The raw and gut-wrenching thoughts of your loved one being gone make it challenging to create a eulogy that truly honors their memory. Moreover, amidst all the chaos, you must gather the courage to stand before a grieving audience, paying tribute to the deceased and offering words of encouragement to those in mourning. The weight of this responsibility can feel like an additional burden atop the mountain of challenges you already face.

However, it is a task that must be undertaken, and if you are reading this, it means that this great responsibility has been entrusted to you. I have personally experienced the position you find yourself in right now, and I wholeheartedly empathize with your situation. Despite the overwhelming emotions you may be experiencing, I firmly believe that you possess bravery and courage, even if you may not feel it at this moment.

About Eulogies

The eulogy is a unique and distinct type of speech that requires a different approach due to many factors, including the mental and emotional state of the audience. This book is specifically designed to assist you in this particular task. It is not a generic speech writing guide, as that is not what you need at this moment. My intention is not to delve into the mechanics of speech writing, but rather to provide you with specific wording, examples and templates that you can adapt, replicate and use to craft your tribute or at least inspire and guide your eulogy writing process.

The body of the eulogy contains crucial sections that we have provided for your convenience. These sections can be customized to suit your specific requirements. Within the eulogies presented in this book, you will find introductions, conclusions, and segments dedicated to sharing cherished memories, highlighting the deceased's passions, discussing their influence, and offering words of comfort to those attending the funeral.

Eulogies employ specific language and sections that enable us to effectively convey the sentiments we wish to express. During challenging times, it can be difficult to find the right words and establish a structure that effectively communicates our emotions while paying tribute to someone who held great significance in our lives.

This book also serves as a guide to help you navigate the grieving process while providing examples and templates for eulogy writing. You can largely copy, modify, and adapt these resources to suit the eulogy you are preparing. Its purpose is to alleviate some of the difficulties associated with this task during such a challenging time.

While these eulogies can serve as sources of inspiration, it is important to personalize your tribute to reflect the unique life and relationship you shared with your loved one. Use the structure and themes highlighted here as guides, but make sure to incorporate your own memories, anecdotes, and emotions to create a heartfelt eulogy that truly honors your loved one.

About Sections, Fields, FAQ and More

Eulogy Sections

This book offers a variety of sections that you can customize and incorporate into your eulogy. The language used in these sections is in line with the common expressions found in eulogies. By eliminating the need to fret over the wording or search for the perfect phrases to express your emotions, writing eulogies becomes a less daunting task.

Fields

We have incorporated specific fields, such as [Name], to conveniently accommodate the inclusion of relevant information about the departed individual. These fields greatly assist in tailoring the eulogies to honor your loved one in a personalized manner.

Tips
Italicized tips are a valuable component designed to ignite creativity and motivation within your writing endeavors. These carefully curated suggestions serve as a catalyst for inspiration, encouraging innovative thinking and the exploration of new ideas.

Prompts
These words serve as a compass for your writing endeavors, urging you to include captivating stories, cherished memories, and entertaining anecdotes.

FAQ
Our Frequently Asked Questions (FAQ) section provides comprehensive answers to common inquiries regarding writing eulogies, as well as coping with loss, healing, and moving forward.

Once again, we extend our deepest condolences to you and your loved ones during this time of need. We sincerely pray that you find the strength to carry on.

1. Section 1 - Violent Crime And Coping With Grief And Loss

1.1 What Is Violent Crime?

Violent crime refers to a category of offenses that pose a direct threat to the safety and well-being of individuals within a society. It encompasses four specific criminal acts, each carrying its own severity and implications. These four distinct offenses are: (1) murder and nonnegligent manslaughter, (2) forcible rape, (3) robbery, and (4) aggravated assault.

1.2 Murder And Nonnegligent Manslaughter

Firstly, we have murder and nonnegligent manslaughter, the most grave and irreversible form of violent crime. This offense involves the intentional killing of another person, often accompanied by malice aforethought or premeditation. The consequences of such acts are devastating, leaving families shattered and communities in mourning.

1.3 Forcible Rape

Next, we encounter forcible rape, an abhorrent act that violates the most fundamental rights of an individual. This offense involves non-consensual sexual intercourse, achieved through the use of force, threats, or coercion. The physical and psychological trauma inflicted upon victims is immeasurable, necessitating a robust response from law enforcement and society as a whole.

1.4 Robbery

Robbery, another component of violent crime, revolves around the unlawful taking of another person's property through force or threat of force. This offense not only results in material loss but also instills fear and insecurity within communities. The act of forcibly depriving individuals of their belongings can have long-lasting effects on their sense of safety and trust in society.

1.5 Aggravated Assault

Lastly, we encounter aggravated assault, a crime characterized by the intentional infliction of severe bodily harm or injury upon another person. This offense often involves the use of weapons or displays a heightened level of violence, posing a significant risk to the physical well-being of victims. The repercussions of such acts extend beyond immediate physical harm, as survivors may suffer from long-term physical and emotional scars.

1.6 Understanding Violent Crime And Loss

Comprehending the essence and constituents of violent crime holds paramount importance for law enforcement agencies, policymakers, and society as a whole. Moreover, it is equally significant for individuals coping with the bereavement and tragic loss of their loved ones due to violent crime.

Enhancing our understanding of violent crime not only aids in the development of effective strategies to combat it but also enables us to create a safer and more secure environment for all members of society. By delving into the intricacies of this issue, we can identify patterns, root causes, and potential preventive measures, thereby empowering law enforcement agencies and policymakers to take proactive steps in curbing the prevalence of violent crime.

Furthermore, comprehending the nature and components of violent crime allows us to provide solace and support to those who have suffered immeasurable loss. By acknowledging the profound impact of violent crime on individuals and communities, we can offer tailored assistance, resources, and counseling to help them navigate the arduous journey of healing and recovery.

1.7 Conclusion

In conclusion, a comprehensive understanding of violent crime is not only a necessity for law enforcement agencies, policymakers, and society at large, but it also serves as a crucial foundation for providing compassion and aid to those affected by such heinous acts. By fostering this understanding, we can work towards a future where violence is minimized, justice is served, and the well-being of all individuals is safeguarded.

2. Navigating The Aftermath Of Violent Crime

2.1 The Impact Of Violent Crime

In the wake of violent crime, individuals and communities are often left grappling with profound feelings of grief, anger, and confusion. The impact of such acts extends far beyond the immediate victims, affecting families, friends, and society at large. This chapter explores the multifaceted nature of violent crime and provides insights into navigating the complex process of dealing with loss.

2.2 Understanding Violent Crime

Violent crime encompasses a wide range of offenses, including assault, homicide, sexual assault, and robbery. Each instance inflicts not only physical harm but also leaves deep emotional scars on those involved. The motives behind such acts vary, from interpersonal conflicts to systemic injustices, but the result is consistently devastating.

2.3 Coping With Loss

The aftermath of violent crime often leaves survivors and loved ones struggling to make sense of their emotions. Grief, in particular, can manifest in myriad ways, from profound sadness to overwhelming rage. It is crucial for individuals to recognize and acknowledge these feelings, allowing themselves the space to mourn and heal.

2.4 Seeking Support

One of the most vital steps in coping with loss is reaching out for support. Whether from friends, family, or professional counselors, having a network of understanding individuals can provide solace and guidance during difficult times. Support groups specifically tailored to survivors of violent crime can offer a sense of community and validation, reminding individuals that they are not alone in their experiences.

2.5 Processing Trauma

The trauma inflicted by violent crime can have long-lasting effects on survivors and witnesses alike. It is essential to prioritize self-care and seek professional help when needed. Therapy modalities such as cognitive-behavioral therapy (CBT) and eye movement desensitization and reprocessing (EMDR) have shown effectiveness in addressing trauma symptoms and facilitating healing.

2.6 Advocating For Change

In the aftermath of a violent crime, many individuals are driven to advocate for systemic change. Whether through legislative action, community organizing, or grassroots activism, channeling grief and anger into positive avenues can be empowering. By working to address the root causes of violence, survivors and allies can honor the memory of those lost while striving to prevent future tragedies.

2.7 Finding Meaning And Hope

Amidst the pain and devastation, there can be moments of profound meaning and hope. Whether through acts of kindness, moments of connection with others, or personal growth and resilience, individuals can find glimmers of light in the darkness. It is essential to hold onto these moments, using them as beacons of hope as one journeys through the process of healing and recovery.

2.8 Conclusion

Dealing with the aftermath of violent crime and loss is a deeply personal and challenging journey. By acknowledging and validating one's emotions, seeking support, and advocating for change, individuals can navigate this difficult terrain with resilience and compassion. Though the scars may never fully heal, there is strength in solidarity and hope for a brighter future.

3. Honoring The Memory Of A Loved One Lost To Criminal Acts

3.1. Introduction: Writing An Emotional Eulogy For Someone Lost To Criminal Acts

Grieving the loss of a loved one is an intensely emotional experience, but when that loss is a result of criminal acts, the pain and complexity of the situation can be overwhelming. Writing a eulogy for someone who has been taken from us in such tragic circumstances requires a delicate balance of remembrance and reflection. In this chapter, we will explore the process of crafting an emotional eulogy that honors the memory of a loved one lost to criminal acts. We will delve into the unique challenges of grieving under these circumstances, discuss ways to capture the essence of the deceased, address the tragic circumstances surrounding their loss, and offer guidance on providing support to the grieving community. Through our words and actions, we can pay tribute to their life, preserve their legacy, and inspire hope amidst the darkness.

3.2 Understanding The Emotional Impact: Processing Grief And Loss

3.2.1 Evaluating The Unique Challenges Of Grieving A Loss To Criminal Acts

Losing someone to criminal acts adds an extra layer of complexity to the grieving process. Not only do we have to grapple with the profound sadness and emptiness of their absence, but we also find ourselves confronting a myriad of other emotions. Anger, frustration, and a sense of injustice often accompany such a loss, making the grieving process even more challenging.

3.2.2 Recognizing The Complex Range Of Emotions

It is important to acknowledge and validate these emotions, understanding that they are a natural response to the circumstances. Allow yourself the space to process these feelings, seeking support from loved ones or professional resources if needed. Remember, there is no right or wrong way to grieve, and everyone experiences it differently. Give yourself permission to feel and heal at your own pace.

3.3 Crafting A Meaningful Narrative: Capturing The Essence Of The Deceased

3.3.1 Reflecting On The Deceased's Personality, Values, And Passions

While the tragedy of their loss may loom large, it is important to remember that the person you are eulogizing lived a life beyond the criminal act that took them away. When crafting your eulogy, take the time to reflect on their personality, values, and passions. What made them unique? What were their dreams and aspirations? By focusing on their life, you honor their memory in a way that transcends the tragic circumstances surrounding their death.

3.3.2 Highlighting Significant Life Events And Achievements

Highlighting significant life events and achievements can also help paint a vivid picture of who they were. Did they have a successful career, create lasting friendships, or contribute to their community? Share stories and anecdotes that showcase their positive impact on the lives of others. Celebrate their accomplishments and the joy they brought to the world.

3.4 Addressing The Tragic Circumstances: Acknowledging The Criminal Acts

3.4.1 Navigating The Sensitivity Of Discussing The Criminal Acts

Addressing the criminal acts that led to their untimely death is an important part of the eulogy, but it requires sensitivity and thoughtfulness. Consider the emotional state of the audience and be mindful of the words you choose. Emphasize the compassion and love your loved one inspired, rather than focusing solely on the tragedy.

3.4.2 Providing Context And Facts Surrounding The Incident

Providing some context and facts surrounding the incident can help others understand the circumstances without dwelling on the gruesome details. Remember, the purpose is to pay tribute to their memory and not to sensationalize or glorify the crime committed against them. Use this opportunity to bring awareness to the issue of criminal acts and advocate for justice, but always keep the focus on celebrating the life that was lost.

3.5 Remembering The Life

3.5.1 Sharing Personal Anecdotes And Memories

Writing an emotional eulogy for someone lost to criminal acts is a challenging task, but it is also an opportunity to honor their memory, share their story, and inspire others to create a more compassionate and just world. Lean on your support network, take your time, and let your words be a testament to the love and resilience that will forever remain in your heart.

3.5.2 Recalling Fond Memories And Stories

When writing a eulogy, it's important to remember that we are not just mourning a person's death, but also celebrating their life. Take the time to share personal anecdotes and memories that bring a smile to your face. Whether it's a funny story from a family gathering or a heartwarming moment shared between friends, these small glimpses into the person's life can help us remember them for who they truly were.

3.5.3 Celebrating The Deceased's Impact On Others

While we may be focusing on our own grief, it's essential to acknowledge the impact the person had on others. Were they a loving partner, a supportive friend, or a mentor who helped shape the lives of many? By celebrating the positive influence they had on those around them, we not only honor their memory but also remind ourselves of the lasting legacy they leave behind.

3.6 Exploring The Impact On Loved Ones: Supporting The Grieving Community

3.6.1 Examining The Emotional Toll On Family And Friends

Losing someone to criminal acts comes with its own set of challenges, as the grief is often mixed with anger and a sense of injustice. Discussing the emotional toll this loss has had on the family and friends can help validate their feelings and provide a space for collective healing. It's important to remind everyone that they are not alone in their pain and that it is okay to experience a range of emotions during this difficult time.

3.6.2 Offering Resources And Support Networks

During times of grief, it can be helpful to point people towards resources and support networks that can assist them in navigating their emotions. This may include grief counseling services, community support groups, or even online forums where individuals going through similar experiences can connect. By providing these valuable resources, you can help ensure that the grieving community has the support they need as they begin their journey towards healing.

3.7 Finding Strength In Unity: Encouraging Resilience And Healing

3.7.1 Fostering A Sense Of Community And Solidarity

In the face of tragedy, finding strength and solace in a supportive community can make a world of difference. Encourage those present to lean on each other during this challenging time by fostering a sense of unity and solidarity. By coming together and supporting one another, we can find comfort and strength in our shared experiences.

3.7.2 Exploring Coping Mechanisms And Healing Strategies

While everyone grieves differently, it can be helpful to explore coping mechanisms and healing strategies that have proven effective for others. This might include engaging in activities that bring joy and solace, seeking professional help if needed, or simply allowing oneself the time and space to process the emotions that arise. Remember, healing takes time, and it's important to remind the grieving community that it's okay to take care of themselves as they navigate their grief.

3.8 Closing Remarks: Leaving A Lasting Tribute And Offering Hope

3.8.1 Creating A Meaningful Conclusion To The Eulogy

As you bring your eulogy to a close, take a moment to reflect on the impact of the person's life and the love they shared with those around them. Craft a meaningful conclusion that encapsulates the essence of who they were and the positive mark they left on the world. A well-crafted ending can provide comfort and closure to those in mourning.

3.8.2 Instilling Hope And Encouraging Positive Change

Finally, in your closing remarks, offer a message of hope and encouragement to the grieving community. Remind them that through the darkness of loss, there is always a glimmer of light. Encourage them to channel their pain into something positive, whether it's advocating for justice, supporting others who have experienced similar loss, or simply spreading kindness and love in honor of the person they've lost. By emphasizing the potential for positive change, you can leave the audience with a sense of hope and a call to action.

3.8.3 Closing Remarks: Leaving A Lasting Tribute And Offering Hope

As we conclude the journey of writing an emotional eulogy for someone lost to criminal acts, let us remember that our words have the power to heal, unite, and inspire. By sharing personal anecdotes, acknowledging the tragedy surrounding their loss, and offering support to the grieving community, we create a meaningful tribute to their life. Let us continue to honor their memory by fostering resilience, finding strength in unity, and working towards a future where such acts of violence become a distant memory. May their legacy serve as a beacon of hope, reminding us to cherish each moment and strive for a world filled with love, compassion, and justice.

4. Crafting The Eulogy: A Step-By-Step Guide To Writing A Meaningful Tribute

4.1 Understanding The Purpose And Structure Of A Eulogy

A eulogy serves as a heartfelt tribute to the person who has passed away. It's an opportunity to reflect on their life, share memories, and celebrate their accomplishments. Understanding the purpose of a eulogy is key to crafting a meaningful tribute.

The structure of a eulogy typically includes an introduction, where you establish your connection to the person and set the tone for the speech. Then, you can delve into different aspects of their life – childhood, achievements, relationships, and so on. Finally, conclude the eulogy by summarizing the impact they had on others and expressing gratitude for the time shared together.

4.2 Gathering Information And Personal Reflections

When writing a eulogy, it's helpful to gather information from various sources: family members, friends, colleagues, and even the person's own writings or speeches. Listen to the stories and anecdotes they share, and reflect on your own personal experiences with the individual.

Take time to recollect specific moments, conversations, or actions that truly exemplify who they were. These personal reflections will add depth and authenticity to your eulogy. Remember, it's not just about listing achievements or accolades – it's about capturing the essence of the person and sharing it with others.

4.3 Organizing And Crafting The Eulogy With Care

With the gathered information and personal reflections in hand, it's time to organize and craft your eulogy. Begin by creating an outline, highlighting the key themes or aspects you want to cover. Then, fill in the details and connect them in a way that flows naturally.

While it's important to be concise, don't be afraid to inject humor or share personal anecdotes that will resonate with the audience. You want the eulogy to feel authentic and true to the person you are honoring. Remember, it's not about impressing others with your writing skills; it's about expressing genuine emotions and capturing the essence of the person's life.

4.4 Leaving A Lasting Legacy And Finding Closure

4.4.1 Reflecting On The Individual's Impact And Legacy

As you bring your eulogy to a close, take a moment to reflect on the person's impact and legacy. Consider the ways in which they touched the lives of others, the positive change they brought to their community, and the lasting memories they created.

Their legacy is not just about the achievements or titles they held, but about the lasting impressions they made on the hearts and minds of those they encountered. By honoring and acknowledging this impact, you help to ensure that their memory lives on.

4.4.2 Finding Closure And Moving Forward With Inspiration

Writing and delivering a eulogy is a cathartic process that allows us to find closure and begin the healing journey. As you conclude your eulogy, remember to offer words of comfort and strength to those in attendance. Share your own commitment to carry forward the values and lessons learned from the person you've lost, finding inspiration in their life to guide you on your own path.

Though the journey may be bittersweet, by celebrating a life full of purpose and passion, we can find solace in knowing that our loved one's memory will continue to inspire us and others for years to come.

4.5 A Celebration Of Life

As we conclude the journey of celebrating a life full of purpose and passion, be reminded of the profound impact one individual can have on the world. Through the process of writing a eulogy, we honor their accomplishments, share cherished memories, and embrace the emotions that come with loss. By delivering a heartfelt tribute, we ensure that their legacy lives on, inspiring others to follow their example of living with purpose and passion. May this act of remembrance bring us closure, while reminding us to seize each day with intention and make a difference in the lives of those around us.

5. Delivering The Eulogy: Tips For Public Speaking And Connecting With The Audience

5.1 Preparing For The Emotional Challenge Of Public Speaking

Public speaking can be an emotional challenge, especially when delivering a eulogy. Take the time to prepare yourself mentally and emotionally before stepping up to the podium. Practice reading the eulogy out loud, allowing yourself to become comfortable with the words and emotions associated with them.

If you feel overwhelmed during the delivery, take deep breaths and remind yourself of the love and admiration you have for the person you are honoring. Embrace the vulnerability of the moment, knowing that sharing your feelings will help others in their own grieving process.

5.2 Engaging The Audience And Establishing A Connection

When delivering a eulogy, it's important to establish a connection with the audience. Speak from the heart, make eye contact, and use body language to convey your emotions. Engage the audience by sharing relatable stories or inviting them to participate in a moment of reflection or remembrance.

Remember, the eulogy is not just for you—it's an opportunity to bring people together, to uplift their spirits, and to honor the person's memory as a collective group. By creating a sense of connection, you can help others find solace, inspiration, and comfort during this difficult time.

5.3 Leaving A Lasting Legacy Through Words

Crafting and delivering a meaningful eulogy is an opportunity to leave a lasting legacy for your loved one. By choosing your words carefully and sharing heartfelt sentiments, you can honor their life and create a lasting impact on those who hear your tribute. Remember that the power of a eulogy lies not only in the memories it evokes but also in the comfort and solace it provides to those who are grieving. Embrace this chance to celebrate a life well-lived and give your loved one a meaningful send-off.

6. Section 2 – Eulogy Examples And Templates

6.1 The Power Of An Empowering Eulogy

When we lose someone dear to us, the pain and grief can be overwhelming. However, amidst the sorrow, there is an opportunity to honor the memory of the departed and create a lasting impact. Writing an empowering eulogy for victims not only allows us to celebrate their lives but also demands change and justice. This section delves into the art of crafting an empowering eulogy, exploring the importance of remembering loved ones and addressing the underlying issues that led to their untimely loss. By harnessing the power of words, personal stories, and advocating for change, we can create meaningful tributes that not only preserve their memories but also inspire a movement towards a more just and compassionate society.

Eulogies are more than just speeches at a funeral; they are a way to celebrate and remember the person we have lost. They provide an opportunity to reflect on their unique qualities, the impact they had on our lives, and the legacies they left behind.

But beyond that, eulogies can also be a platform for demanding change and justice, especially in cases where the loss was a result of injustice, violence, or systemic issues.

In this section, we will explore how to write an empowering eulogy for victims, focusing on celebrating their lives and demanding the necessary changes to prevent similar tragedies in the future.

May these eulogies serve as a guiding light for those who find themselves faced with the daunting task of crafting and delivering a eulogy for a loved one lost to crime.

7. Eulogy 1 - Preserving Memories, Demanding Change: Writing An Empowering Eulogy For Victims

7.1 Introduction And Reflection

7.1.1 Remembering And Celebrating A Life Cut Short

Today, we gather with profound sorrow to bid farewell to [Name], whose life was tragically and abruptly taken from us by an act of senseless violence. I am [Your Name], [Name]'s [Your relationship to the deceased], and it is with great honor that I stand before you today, representing the cherished individuals who have come together in this solemn moment.

7.1.2 Reflecting On [Name]'s Unique Qualities And Contributions

[Name] was a remarkable person who brought so much joy and inspiration to those around [him/her/them]. Whether it was [his/her/their] infectious laughter, [his/her/their] unwavering kindness, or [his/her/their] passion for making a difference in the world, [Name] had a unique set of qualities that made [him/her/them] stand out.

[*Tip: Reflecting on these qualities allows us to remember the essence of who they were and the impact they had on our lives.*]

[**Prompt:** Provide examples or stories that show the qualities, essence or contributions of your loved one.]

7.2 The Legacy And Shared Experiences

7.2.1 The Loved Ones Who Continue The Legacy

Our beloved [Name]'s passing has left a profound void in our lives. In reflecting on [his/her/their] life, it is important to acknowledge those who continue to carry on [his/her/their] legacy. [Name] is survived by [State and name the close kins e.g.{ [his/her/their] loving family, including [his/her/their] devoted [husband/wife/spouse], [Name] and their [number] children [List Names], who were the center of [his/her/their] universe.}] [State and name other relatives e.g.{ [He/She/They] leave(s) behind a host of cherished relatives, including nieces, nephews, and cousins whom [he/she/they] held dear.]} Additionally, [he/she/they] touched the lives of countless friends and acquaintances through [his/her/their] graciousness and unwavering support. [His/Her/Their] presence will be greatly missed by all who had the privilege of knowing [him/her/them]. In the face of this immense sorrow that has befallen us, we seek solace in the profound realization that [Name] has left an indelible mark on the lives of those fortunate enough to have encountered [his/her/their] limitless love and contagious joy.

7.2.2 Fond Memories And Shared Experiences

As we recall [Name]'s life, it is important to cherish the memories and experiences we shared with [him/her/them]. Whether it was the adventures we embarked on together, the inside jokes we laughed about, or the quiet moments of connection we shared, these memories are a testament to the depth of our relationship.

[*Tip: Sharing these fond memories during a eulogy not only keeps your loved one's spirit alive but also brings comfort and unity to those who are mourning their loss.*]

[**Prompt:** Include a story about a memory or experience shared with your loved one - One that shows their adventurous or fun side.]

7.3 Understanding The Impact: The Need For Change

7.3.1 Examining The Circumstances And Causes Of [Name]'s Loss

[*Tip: It is essential to examine the circumstances and causes of [Name]'s tragic loss. Understanding the events that led to their passing helps us make sense of the situation and recognize any injustices or failures that occurred. By shining a light on these factors, we can bring attention to the need for change and prevent similar incidents from happening in the future.*]

[**Prompt:** State with compassion, clarity and brevity the events that led to the passing of your loved one.]

7.3.2 Recognizing The Broader Patterns And Systemic Issues

[*Tip: Sometimes, the loss of a loved one highlights larger patterns and systemic issues that need to be addressed. [Name]'s story may not be an isolated incident, but rather a reflection of a wider problem within our society. It is crucial to recognize these patterns and call for systemic changes that will prevent others from suffering the same fate.*]

[**Prompt:** Identify and advocate for change to systemic issues that contribute to crime and violence.]

7.4 Crafting An Empowering Eulogy: Honoring Strength And Resilience

7.4.1 Identifying Key Themes And Messages

[*Tip: When crafting an empowering eulogy for someone like [Name], it is important to identify key themes and messages that will resonate with the audience. These themes could include strength, resilience, justice, or the pursuit of positive change. By focusing on these messages, we can honor [Name]'s memory and inspire others to take action.*]

7.4.2 Highlighting Personal Achievements And Overcoming Challenges

[*Tip: In addition to celebrating [Name]'s qualities and contributions, highlighting their personal achievements and their ability to overcome challenges can inspire others facing similar struggles.*]

41

[**Prompt:** Share stories of their resilience and determination to remind everyone of the strength within us and encourage them to keep fighting for a better world.]

7.5 Sharing Personal Stories: Capturing Memories And Inspiring Change

[*Tip: When saying goodbye to a loved one, one of the most powerful ways to honor their memory is by sharing personal stories. Encouraging friends and family to come together and reminisce about the moments they shared with the person who has passed away can be both cathartic and uplifting. These stories capture the essence of who they were, the impact they had on others, and the memories that will forever be cherished.*]

[**Prompt:** Share stories that highlight the character and uniqueness of your loved one and how they impacted your life.]

7.5.1 Encouraging Friends And Family To Share Their Stories

[*Tip: In times of grief, it can be difficult to find the right words to express our feelings. However, by encouraging friends and family to share their stories, we create a safe space for remembrance and healing. Whether it's a funny anecdote, a heartwarming memory, or a lesson learned, these stories help keep the spirit of our loved ones alive.*]

7.5.2 Exploring The Impact Of Personal Narratives In Generating Empathy And Understanding

[*Tip: Personal narratives have a unique power to generate empathy and understanding. As we share stories about our loved ones, we invite others into their world, allowing them to see the person behind the tragedy. These stories humanize victims and help others connect with their experiences on a deeper level. By sharing personal narratives, we can inspire change and foster a sense of collective responsibility to prevent similar injustices from occurring in the future.*]

7.6 Addressing Injustice: Demanding Accountability And Awareness

[*Tip: Writing an empowering eulogy goes beyond mere remembrance; it also serves as a platform to address the injustice that led to the loss of our loved one's life. By demanding accountability and raising awareness about the underlying issues, we can bring attention to the injustices that need to be rectified.*]

7.6.1 Advocating For Justice And Holding Responsible Parties Accountable

[*Tip: An empowering eulogy should not shy away from addressing the need for justice. By advocating for a thorough investigation, demanding accountability from responsible parties, and supporting legal proceedings, we can strive to ensure that those who caused harm are held responsible for their actions. This pursuit of justice can provide closure and a sense of vindication for both the deceased and their grieving loved ones.*]

7.6.2 Raising Awareness About The Underlying Issues And Seeking Support

[*Tip: To effect lasting change, an empowering eulogy must also raise awareness about the underlying issues that contributed to the tragedy. Whether it is systemic racism, mental health stigmatization, or any other pertinent issue, we can shed light on these topics and encourage others to join in the fight for change. By seeking support from organizations, communities, and individuals who share our goals, we can form a united front in the pursuit of justice and prevention.*]

7.7 Moving Forward: Creating Lasting Change In [Name]'s Memory

[*Tip: In the face of grief, it may seem challenging to find a path forward. However, an empowering eulogy can serve as a catalyst for action and lasting change in the memory of our loved ones.*]

7.7.1 Channeling Grief Into Positive Action

[*Tip: Grief can be overwhelming, but channeling it into positive action can be transformative. Through these actions, we can turn tragedy into an opportunity for growth, healing, and empowerment.*]

[**Prompt:** Channel your grief and anger into productive endeavors, such as volunteering, advocating, to honor our loved one and create tangible change.]

7.7.2 Establishing Foundations Or Initiatives To Promote Change

[*Tip: Another way to preserve the legacy of our loved ones is by establishing foundations or initiatives dedicated to promoting change. These initiatives can serve as catalysts for action.*]

[**Prompt:** Create platforms that address the issues close to your hearts, to continue the fight for justice and inspire others to join in making a difference.]

7.8 Conclusion: The Legacy Of An Empowering Eulogy

[*Tip: An empowering eulogy has the power to preserve not only the memory of our loved ones but also their impact on the world. By sharing personal stories, demanding accountability, raising awareness, and taking action, we can ensure that their legacy inspires positive change.*]

7.8.1 Farewell And Closing

In bidding our final farewell to [Name], we are reminded that [his/her/their] impact transcends [his/her/their] physical presence. As we honor and remember [his/her/their] legacy, we must commit ourselves to continue the work necessary to prevent similar incidents. Whether it is through advocating for justice, amplifying marginalized voices, or fighting for equality, let us be inspired by [Name]'s impact and potential that was snuffed out needlessly. By carrying forward in love, we can ensure that [his/her/their] memory lives on and strive to create a world where every precious life is valued and protected.

8. Eulogy 2 - A Eulogy For Someone Lost To Violent Crime

8.1 Introduction And Greeting

Ladies and gentlemen,

Today, we gather with heavy hearts to bid farewell to [Name], whose life was tragically cut short by an act of senseless violence. I am [Your Name], [Name]'s [Your relationship to the deceased] and I am honored to speak on behalf of the loved ones gathered here today. We stand here not only to mourn [his/her/their] untimely departure but also to celebrate the beautiful soul that graced our lives and left an indelible mark on our hearts.

8.2 The Loved Ones Who Continue The Legacy

Our beloved [Name]'s passing has left a profound void in our lives. In reflecting on [his/her/their] life, it is important to acknowledge those who continue to carry on [his/her/their] legacy. [Name] is survived by [State and name the close kins e.g.{ [his/her/their] loving family, including [his/her/their] devoted [husband/wife/spouse], [Name] and their [number] children [List Names], who were the center of [his/her/their] universe.]}

[State and name other relatives e.g.{ [He/She/They] leave(s) behind a host of cherished relatives, including nieces, nephews, and cousins whom [he/she/they] held dear.]} Additionally, [he/she/they] touched the lives of countless friends and acquaintances through [his/her/their] graciousness and unwavering support. [His/Her/Their] presence will be greatly missed by all who had the privilege of knowing [him/her/them]. Even though this loss brings us immeasurable sadness, we take comfort in the knowledge that [Name] has left a lasting impact on the lives of those whom [he/she/their] lovingly touched with joy and happiness.

8.3 Remembering The Life We Lost

[Name] was more than just a victim of circumstance; [he/she/they] [was/were] a beacon of light in our lives, a source of joy, love, and inspiration. [His/Her/Their] infectious laughter, compassionate spirit, and unwavering kindness touched the lives of all who were fortunate enough to know [him/her/them]. [His/Her/Their] presence lit up the room, and [his/her/their] absence leaves a void that can never be filled.

8.4 Sharing Stories That Highlight The Impact Or Beloved Had On Us

[**Prompt:** Share stories that highlight the character and uniqueness of your loved one and how he/she/they impacted your life.]

8.5 Expressing Grief

It's impossible to comprehend the depth of grief and pain that [Name]'s loved ones are experiencing right now. Losing someone we cherish to such a senseless act of violence is an unfathomable tragedy that shakes us to our core. But amidst the darkness, let us not forget the light that [Name] brought into our lives.

8.6 The Impact Of Our Loved One

[He/She/They] [was/were] a friend, a sibling, a child, a partner—a cherished member of our community whose memory will live on in the countless lives [he/she/they] touched. Though [he/she/they] may no longer be physically present with us, [his/her/their] spirit will continue to shine brightly through the memories we hold dear and the love we carry in our hearts.

8.7 Reflection On The Implications Of Violence

As we mourn the loss of [Name], let us also reflect on the broader implications of violence in our society. Let us strive to create a world where every individual can live free from fear, where compassion and empathy prevail over hatred and cruelty. Let us honor [Name]'s memory by working towards a future where no family has to endure the pain of losing a loved one to violence.

8.8 Closing With Compassion

In closing, let us take solace in the cherished memories we shared with [Name] and the profound impact [he/she/they] had on our lives. Though [his/her/their] time with us was cut short, [his/her/their] legacy of love, kindness, and compassion will endure for eternity. May [he/she/they] rest in peace, knowing that [his/her/their] light will continue to shine brightly in our hearts forevermore.

Thank you.

9. Eulogy 3 - A Eulogy For A Relative Lost To Violent Crime

9.1 Introduction And Greeting

Ladies and gentlemen,

We gather here today with heavy hearts, united in both grief and remembrance as we bid farewell to [Name], a soul taken from us far too soon by the senseless hand of violence. I am [Your Name], [Name]'s [Your relationship to the deceased] and I am honored to speak on behalf of the loved ones gathered here today.

9.2 The Loved Ones Who Continue The Legacy

Our beloved [Name]'s passing has left a profound void in our lives. In reflecting on [his/her/their] life, it is important to acknowledge those who continue to carry on [his/her/their] legacy. [Name] is survived by [State and name the close kins e.g.{ [his/her/their] loving family, including [his/her/their] devoted [husband/wife/spouse], [Name] and their [number] children [List Names], who were the center of [his/her/their] universe.]} [State and name other relatives e.g.{ [He/She/They] leave(s) behind a host of cherished relatives, including nieces, nephews, and cousins whom [he/she/they] held dear.]} Additionally, [he/she/they] touched the lives of countless friends and acquaintances through [his/her/their] graciousness and unwavering support. [His/Her/Their] presence will be greatly missed by all who had the privilege of knowing [him/her/them]. Even though this loss brings us immeasurable sadness, we take comfort in the knowledge that [Name] has left a lasting impact on the lives of those whom [he/she/their] lovingly touched with joy and happiness.

9.3 The Impact Of Our Beloved

[Name] was more than a mere victim of circumstance; [he/she/they] were a beacon of light in our lives, a source of joy, love, and inspiration. As we reflect on [his/her/their] life, we are reminded of the warmth [he/she/they] brought into every room, the laughter that echoed in [his/her/their] presence, and the love that flowed from [his/her/their] heart.

[**Prompt:** Share stories that show the impact your loved one had on your life.]

9.4 Memories Of Our Beloved

[His/Her/Their] memory will forever be etched in our minds, a reminder of the preciousness of life and the fragility of our existence. In the wake of this tragedy, we are left grappling with questions that may never find answers, with wounds that may never fully heal. But amidst the pain, let us also find solace in the beautiful memories we shared with [Name], in the love that continues to bind us together.

[**Prompt:** Share stories that highlight the character and uniqueness of your loved one.]

[Name] may have been taken from us unjustly, but [his/her/their] spirit lives on in the lives [he/she/they] touched, in the hearts [he/she/they] filled with love and kindness. Let us carry forward [his/her/their] legacy, embodying the values [he/she/they] held dear – compassion, forgiveness, and resilience.

9.5 Plea For Justice

Though we mourn [his/her/their] passing, let us also celebrate the life [he/she/they] lived, the impact [he/she/they] made, and the love [he/she/they] shared. And as we say our final goodbyes, let us hold onto the hope that justice will prevail, that peace will someday find its way into our hearts.

9.6 Finding Closure: Cherishing The Memories

Rest in peace, dear [Name]. Your light will continue to shine brightly in our memories, guiding us through the darkness, reminding us to cherish every moment we have together.

May you find eternal peace and serenity in the embrace of the heavens.

Amen.

10. Eulogy 4 - A Tribute For A Relative That Died By Homicide

Writing a tribute for a loved one who died by homicide is a deeply personal and emotional task. Here's a heartfelt example of a tribute that inspires others to use their words to shine a light on injustices and demand a better future for all.

10.1 Introduction And Greeting

Today is a somber occasion as we gather in loving memory of [Name]. I am [Your Name], [Name]'s [Your relationship to the deceased] and I am honored to speak on behalf of the loved ones gathered here today.

[Name] was more than a family member; [he/she/they] were a shining light in our lives, a beacon of joy, kindness, and love. [His/Her/Their] life was tragically cut short by an act of senseless violence, leaving an indelible void in our hearts and our family.

10.2 The Impact And Legacy

Today, as we gather to honor the life of [Name], we are reminded of the profound impact [he/she/they] had on each and every one of us. [Name] leaves behind a legacy woven with love, laughter, and cherished memories. [His/Her/Their] presence touched the lives of not only family members but also countless friends who became an extension of [his/her/their] family. Through the bonds of friendship and the ties of kinship, [Name] created a network of support and affection that will endure beyond this moment of sorrow. Though [he/she/they] may no longer walk beside us, [his/her/their] spirit will forever live on in the hearts of those [he/she/they] leave(s) behind.

1.0.3 The Character And Nature Of The Beloved

[Name] had an infectious laughter that could brighten even the darkest of days. [His/Her/Their] presence filled every room with warmth and compassion. [He/She/They] [was/were] the embodiment of selflessness, always putting others' needs before [his/her/their] own, and [his/her/their] generosity knew no bounds.

[**Prompt:** Share stories that highlight the character and uniqueness of your loved one and how they impacted your life.]

10.4 Remembering The Spirit Of The Beloved

Though the circumstances of [his/her/their] passing are painful and difficult to comprehend, we choose to remember [Name] for the beautiful soul [he/she/they] were and the countless memories [he/she/they] gifted us. [His/Her/Their] spirit will forever live on in the cherished moments we shared together, in the love [he/she/they] bestowed upon us, and in the legacy of kindness [he/she/they] leave behind.

10.5 Cherishing The Moment

As we mourn the loss of [Name], we also reflect on the importance of cherishing every moment with those we hold dear. Let us honor [Name]'s memory by spreading love, kindness, and compassion in our own lives, and by advocating for a world where senseless acts of violence have no place.

10.6 Closing And Remembering The Life Of The Beloved

Though [Name] may no longer walk beside us, [his/her/their] light will continue to guide us through the darkness. [He/She/They] will forever remain in our hearts, a cherished presence that neither time nor distance can diminish.

Rest in peace, dear [Name]. You are loved beyond measure and missed more than words can express. Until we meet again.

[**Prompt:** Feel free to personalize this tribute with specific memories, qualities, or sentiments that resonate with your loved one. Remember, there's no right or wrong way to honor their memory. Allow yourself to express your grief and celebrate their life in a way that feels meaningful to you and your family.]

11. Eulogy 5 - For One Who Carried The Torch Of Justice

11.1 Introduction And Greeting

11.1.1 Honoring The Legacy

Today we gather to pay tribute to the remarkable life and profound impact of [Name]. I am [Your Name], [Name]'s [Your relationship to the deceased] and I am honored to speak on behalf of the loved ones gathered here today. As we reflect on [Name]'s untimely passing, we are compelled to remember the accomplishments, values, and unwavering commitment to justice that defined [his/her/their] existence. Through a heartfelt eulogy, we seek to celebrate [Name]'s legacy, explore the ways in which [he/she/they] influenced society, and inspire others to carry on [his/her/their] torch of justice. Join us as we delve into the life of a remarkable individual who left an indelible mark on the world.

11.1.2 The Loved Ones And Legacy

Our beloved [Name]'s passing has left a profound void in our lives. In reflecting on [his/her/their] life, it is important to acknowledge those who continue to carry on [his/her/their] legacy. [Name] is survived by [State and name the close kins e.g.{ [his/her/their] loving family, including [his/her/their] devoted [husband/wife/spouse], [Name] and their [number] children [List Names], who were the center of [his/her/their] universe.]} [State and name other relatives e.g.{ [He/She/They] leave(s) behind a host of cherished relatives, including nieces, nephews, and cousins whom [he/she/they] held dear.]} Additionally, [he/she/they] touched the lives of countless friends and acquaintances through [his/her/their] graciousness and unwavering support. [His/Her/Their] presence will be greatly missed by all who had the privilege of knowing [him/her/them]. Even though this loss brings us immeasurable sadness, we take comfort in the knowledge that [Name] has left a lasting impact on the lives of those whom [he/she/their] lovingly touched with joy and happiness.

11.2 Remembering Achievements: Early Life And Background

11.2.2 Education And Professional Journey

To understand the depth of [Name]'s impact, we must delve into [his/her/their] life story. From humble beginnings, [Name] persevered through life's challenges and emerged as a beacon of inspiration for all. From [his/her/their] early days, where every hurdle only fueled [his/her/their] determination, to a remarkable educational journey that sharpened [his/her/their] intellect, [Name] grew into an individual who would leave an indelible mark on the world.

11.2.3 Notable Accomplishments And Contributions

Through [his/her/their] passion, hard work, and unwavering dedication, [Name] achieved several notable accomplishments. [His/Her/Their] contributions in [specific field/industry] have revolutionized the way we perceive [specific field/industry], making [him/her/them] an icon in [his/her/their] own right. [Name]'s legacy will forever be intertwined with [his/her/their] significant achievements, serving as a testament to [his/her/their] brilliance and tenacity.

11.3 Reflecting On The Impact Of [Name]'s Loss On Society

11.3.1 The Shockwave of Grief: Community Response

The loss of [Name] has sent shockwaves throughout our community, leaving us grappling with a profound sense of grief. [His/Her/Their] departure has created a void impossible to fill, as [his/her/their] absence has left an unmistakable mark on our collective consciousness. Friends, colleagues, and loved ones have come together to mourn the loss of someone who has touched countless lives.

11.3.2 Examining The Void Left Behind

As we reflect on this immeasurable loss, we cannot ignore the impact [Name] had on society as a whole. [His/Her/Their] absence not only leaves a void in our hearts, but it also creates a void in the pursuit of justice, compassion, and progress. We must now find the strength to carry [his/her/their] torch of justice forward, as we honor [his/her/their] memory by continuing the work [he/she/they] began.

11.4 Uncovering [Name]'s Passion For Justice And Advocacy

11.4.1 The Roots of [Name]'s Commitment To Justice

One of the most defining aspects of [Name]'s life was [his/her/their] unwavering commitment to justice and advocacy. Rooted in [his/her/their] own experiences and a deep sense of empathy, [Name] made it [his/her/their] life's mission to fight for the rights of the marginalized and voiceless. [His/Her/Their] passion ignited a fire within, propelling [him/her/them] to champion various causes and become a symbol of hope for those in need.

11.4.2 Major Areas Of Advocacy And Activism

From advocating for social equality to tirelessly working towards environmental preservation, [Name] took on multiple arenas of activism. [His/Her/Their] dedication and ability to inspire change have influenced countless individuals to stand up, speak out, and make a tangible impact on the world. [Name]'s efforts in [specific areas of advocacy] have undoubtedly set a precedent for those who continue to fight for justice.

As we bid farewell to [Name], let us not only mourn [his/her/their] loss but also celebrate the life [he/she/they] led and the transformative impact [he/she/they] had on our world. May we be inspired by [his/her/their] legacy to continue the pursuit of justice, compassion, and progress, carrying [his/her/their] torch forward as a tribute to [his/her/their] incredible spirit.

11.5 The Power Of [Name]'s Voice: Inspiring Change Through Words

11.5.1 Influential Speeches And Public Addresses

[Name] possessed an extraordinary ability to captivate audiences with [his/her/their] words. Whether speaking to a small gathering or addressing a crowd of thousands, [his/her/their] powerful speeches moved hearts and ignited a sense of purpose. [His/Her/Their] ability to articulate complex issues in a way that resonated with people from all walks of life was truly remarkable. Through [his/her/their] speeches, [Name] challenged societal norms, exposed injustices, and called for unity and equality. [His/Her/Their] words continue to inspire change and remind us of the power we all possess to create a more just world.

11.5.2 Impactful Writing And Publications

Beyond [his/her/their] compelling speeches, [Name] also left an indelible mark through [his/her/their] writing. [His/Her/Their] publications delved deep into the heart of social issues, shedding light on hidden truths and offering unique perspectives. [Name]'s words had the power to educate, enlighten, and provoke thought.

[His/Her/Their] articles, essays, and books continue to be revered as powerful tools for change. Through [his/her/their] writing, [Name] challenged conventional wisdom and sparked conversations that would shape our understanding of justice and equality. [His/Her/Their] words remain as a testament to [his/her/their] unwavering commitment to creating a better world for all.

11.6 Lessons Learned: Carrying Forward [Name]'s Legacy Of Justice

11.6.1 Core Values And Principles

To honor [Name]'s legacy, it is crucial that we embrace the core values and principles [he/she/they] stood for. [Name] believed in the inherent worth and dignity of every individual, championed equality and justice, and fought tirelessly against oppression in all its forms. By embodying these values in our own lives, we keep [Name]'s spirit alive and ensure [his/her/their] impact continues to resonate.

11.6.2 Incorporating [Name]'s Methods And Strategies

In addition to [his/her/their] values, [Name] employed specific methods and strategies that proved highly effective in the pursuit of justice. Whether it was grassroots organizing, peaceful protests, or strategic advocacy, [Name] understood the importance of taking action and making [his/her/their] voice heard. By adopting and adapting these methods, we can carry forward [Name]'s legacy, amplifying [his/her/their] efforts and advancing the cause of justice.

11.7 A Call To Action: Empowering Others To Make A Difference

11.7.1 Encouraging Civic Engagement

[Name] believed that change begins with individuals who are willing to stand up and take action. [He/She/They] understood the power of collective voices coming together to challenge the status quo. To honor [Name]'s memory, we must encourage and empower others to engage in civic activism. By participating in community initiatives, advocating for change, and using our voices to speak out against injustice, we can drive positive and lasting impact.

11.7.2 Supporting Organizations And Movements [Name] Believed In

[Name] was deeply passionate about numerous organizations and movements dedicated to justice and equality. To carry [Name]'s torch, it is vital that we support these causes and contribute to their continued success. Whether through donations, volunteering, or spreading awareness, our efforts can help these organizations thrive and bring about meaningful change in the world.

11.8 Conclusion: Keeping [Name]'s Torch Of Justice Burning

11.8.1 Ensuring [Name]'s Impact Endures

Though [Name] may no longer be with us, [his/her/their] impact and legacy lives on. It is our responsibility to keep [his/her/their] torch of justice burning brightly. By embracing [his/her/their] values and principles, incorporating [his/her/their] methods and strategies, encouraging civic engagement and activism, and supporting the organizations [Name] believed in, we can ensure that [his/her/their] unwavering pursuit of justice continues to inspire and effect change. Let us carry forward [Name]'s torch with passion, determination, and an unwavering commitment to building a more just and equitable world for all.

12. Section 3 - Understanding, Coping And Healing From Loss Due To Crime And Violence

When we lose someone dear to us, it can feel like the world has been turned upside down. The pain and grief can be overwhelming, leaving us searching for ways to find solace and healing. In times like these, eulogies play a crucial role in honoring the memory of our loved ones while also providing us with a path towards healing.

In this section we discuss the role and techniques of therapy in the healing process. We also consider the power of forgiveness in helping to find closure. We discuss ways that support can be beneficial and its importance in learning to cope. We hope that you find solace in the information provided here and most of all we want to let you know that you are not alone in this period of loss. Your situation may be unique to you but the feelings of loss and hurt are not dissimilar from all who have lost loved ones to crime. Know that healing from this loss is not only possible but probable with patience, support, recovery techniques and therapy if necessary.

13. Crime And Violence-The Lasting Impact On Individuals, Families, And Communities

13.1 Introduction: The Profound Impact

13.1.1 Remembering The Beloved Lost

Crime and violence have a profound impact on our communities, leaving behind shattered lives and grief-stricken families. This chapter serves as a solemn reminder of the lives cut short, the dreams left unfulfilled, and the enduring pain endured by their loved ones. In this reflection, we delve into the far-reaching consequences of crime and violence, examine the broken justice system, and seek ways to empower communities in their fight against these pervasive issues. Above all, we honor the memory of those we have lost by inspiring meaningful change in our societies.

13.1.2 The Importance Of Honoring And Remembering

In a world plagued by crime and violence, it is important to take a moment to remember and honor those we have lost. Each life cut short is not a mere statistic or a news headline; it represents a unique story, a cherished individual who left an indelible mark on the lives of those around them. By acknowledging their lives and the impact they had, we not only pay tribute to the departed but also remind ourselves of the need for a safer and more compassionate society.

13.2 Tracing The Impact Of Crime And Violence On Communities

13.2.1 Understanding The Ripple Effects Of Crime And Violence

When crime and violence strike a community, the repercussions extend far beyond the immediate victims. The shockwaves reverberate through families, friends, and neighbors, leaving a lasting impact on the collective psyche. Fear and mistrust may infiltrate once tight-knit communities, altering the way people interact and undermining the sense of security that is essential for individual and communal well-being.

13.2.2 Social And Economic Consequences

Beyond the emotional toll, crime and violence take a heavy toll on society as a whole. Communities plagued by high levels of crime often suffer from a decreased quality of life, hindering economic growth and development. Businesses may shy away from investing in areas deemed unsafe, exacerbating unemployment and poverty. The social fabric frays, leading to a cycle of despair that can be difficult to break. It is essential to address these underlying issues and work towards fostering safer and more prosperous environments.

13.3 Celebrating The Life And Legacy Of The Departed

13.3.1 Sharing Stories And Memories

In the face of tragedy, it becomes even more crucial to celebrate the lives of those we have lost. Sharing stories and memories not only keeps their spirit alive but also helps loved ones find solace in the collective remembrance. As we recount the anecdotes and experiences that made them who they were, we realize the profound impact they had on our lives, and we find strength in the lasting connections that death cannot sever.

13.3.2 Achievements And Contributions

Every life, no matter how brief, is marked by significant moments and achievements. Whether it's academic, professional, or personal accomplishments, it is important to honor and recognize the contributions the departed made during their time with us. By celebrating their achievements, we acknowledge the positive imprint they left behind and inspire others to strive for greatness in their own lives.

13.4 Examining The Toll Of Crime And Violence On Families And Loved Ones

13.4.1 The Journey Of Grief And Loss

The burden of loss weighs heavily on the families and loved ones left behind. Grief is a complex and deeply personal journey, marked by a range of emotions such as shock, anger, and profound sadness. It is important for society to provide the necessary support systems and resources for those affected by crime and violence, enabling them to begin the healing process and find hope in the midst of despair.

13.4.2 Coping-Trauma And Its Aftermath

The trauma experienced by those affected by crime and violence can have long-lasting effects. It is imperative to acknowledge and address the psychological scars left behind. By providing access to mental health services and fostering a culture of empathy and understanding, we can take significant strides towards helping individuals and communities cope with the aftermath of such tragedies. Together, we can turn pain into resilience and build a future where crime and violence no longer steal our loved ones away.

13.5 Reflecting On The Broken Justice System And Its Consequences

13.5.1 Flaws Within The Justice System

In a world where justice is supposed to be blind, it often feels like it has one eye open and a hand tied behind its back. Our justice system, once thought to be the protector of the innocent and the punisher of the guilty, is riddled with flaws that allow criminals to slip through the cracks. From overcrowded prisons to biased sentencing, it's clear that we have a long way to go in achieving true justice for all.

13.5.2 The Impact-Victims And Communities

When the scales of justice become imbalanced, it is the victims and communities who suffer the most. Families left in the wake of violence and crime are left to pick up the shattered pieces of their lives, while communities are plagued by fear. The consequences of a broken justice system are far-reaching and can linger for generations, leaving scars that are not easily healed.

13.6 Empowering Communities To Combat Crime And Violence

13.6.1 Community Engagement And Unity

They say it takes a village to raise a child, but it also takes a village to combat crime and violence. Communities must come together, united in their determination to take back their streets. By fostering a sense of belonging and connection, we can create an environment where crime and violence have no place to thrive. It's time to put the "neighbor" back in neighborhood and reclaim our communities.

13.6.2 Effective Crime Prevention Strategies

Prevention is always better than cure, and the same holds true for crime and violence. It's not just about reacting to incidents; it's about taking proactive measures to prevent them from happening in the first place. From implementing community policing programs to tackling the root causes of crime, we need to invest in strategies that address the problem at its core. By doing so, we can build a safer and more secure future for all.

13.7 Providing Support And Healing For Survivors Of Crime And Violence

13.7.1 Accessing Support Services For Victims And Families

When tragedy strikes, it's crucial that survivors of crime and violence have access to the support services they need to heal and move forward. From counseling and therapy to legal assistance, these services can provide a lifeline for those struggling to cope with the aftermath of trauma. It is our duty to ensure that survivors and their families have the resources and support they need to rebuild their lives.

13.7.2 Advocating For Trauma-Informed Care And Rehabilitation

Healing is a process, and it requires more than just physical recovery. We must advocate for trauma-informed care and rehabilitation for victims of crime and violence. By understanding the long-term effects of trauma and providing comprehensive support, we can help survivors regain their strength and find a path towards healing. It's time to shift the narrative from just punishment to rehabilitation, giving every individual the chance to rebuild and thrive.

13.8 Conclusion: Honoring The Memory And Inspiring Change

13.8.1 Remembering The Beloved Lost As Catalysts For Change

As we bid farewell to those beloved ones lost to crime and violence, let us remember them not only as victims but also as catalysts for change. Their stories should ignite within us a fierce determination to fight for justice and advocate for a better world. We owe it to them and ourselves to carry their memory forward and strive for a society where crime and violence are no longer the norm.

13.8.2 Building Safer Communities

In the face of adversity, we must come together and commit ourselves to building safer and stronger communities. It's time to address the flaws within our justice system, empower our neighborhoods, and provide the necessary support and healing for survivors. By taking collective action, we can create a society that stands up against crime and violence and works tirelessly towards a future where every person feels safe and protected. Let us honor those we have lost by creating lasting change.

14. Therapy And Coping With Violent Crime And Loss

14.1 Therapy And Coping Strategies

Therapy and coping strategies for individuals affected by violent crime and loss are crucial for their healing and well-being. Here are some approaches commonly used by therapists and counselors:

14.2 Trauma-Focused Therapy

Therapies such as Cognitive Behavioral Therapy (CBT), Eye Movement Desensitization and Reprocessing (EMDR), and Trauma-focused Cognitive Behavioral Therapy (TF-CBT) can help individuals process traumatic experiences, manage distressing symptoms, and develop coping mechanisms.

14.3 Grief Counseling

Grief counseling provides a safe space for individuals to express their emotions, navigate the stages of grief (denial, anger, bargaining, depression, acceptance), and find meaning in their loss. Support groups can also be beneficial, connecting individuals with others who have experienced similar losses.

14.4 Mindfulness And Relaxation Techniques

Practices like mindfulness meditation, deep breathing exercises, and progressive muscle relaxation can help individuals manage anxiety, reduce stress, and promote a sense of calmness.

14.5 Expressive Therapies

Art therapy, music therapy, and other forms of creative expression can serve as outlets for processing emotions, exploring difficult experiences, and fostering self-expression in non-verbal ways.

14.6 Cognitive Restructuring

This involves challenging and reframing negative thought patterns related to the traumatic event or loss, promoting more adaptive coping strategies and beliefs.

14.7 Safety Planning

For individuals who may still be at risk or experiencing ongoing safety concerns, safety planning can help them identify and implement strategies to protect themselves and their loved ones.

14.8 Building Support Networks

Encouraging individuals to reach out to friends, family members, and other supportive individuals can provide invaluable emotional support and practical assistance during difficult times.

14.9 Self-Care Practices

Engaging in self-care activities such as exercise, healthy eating, adequate sleep, and engaging in hobbies can help individuals maintain their physical and emotional well-being.

14.10 Setting Realistic Goals

Setting small, achievable goals can provide a sense of accomplishment and progress, even in the face of overwhelming challenges.

14.11 Seeking Professional Help

Encouraging individuals to seek professional help from therapists, counselors, or support organizations specialized in trauma and grief can provide them with the guidance and support they need to navigate their healing journey.

It's important to recognize that everyone copes with trauma and loss differently, and what works for one person may not work for another. Therefore, therapy should be tailored to meet the individual's unique needs and preferences. Additionally, it's essential to prioritize safety and seek immediate help if someone is in danger or experiencing a mental health crisis.

15. Understanding The Concept Of Forgiveness In Coping With Loss Caused By Violent Crime

15.1 Introduction: Exploring The Significance Of Forgiveness In Coping With Loss After Violent Crime

In the aftermath of a violent crime, the grieving process can be overwhelming, leaving individuals and communities grappling with pain, anger, and a deep sense of loss. While finding healing and closure may seem like an insurmountable challenge, the concept of forgiveness emerges as a powerful tool in coping with the aftermath of such traumatic events. This chapter delves into the significance of forgiveness, shedding light on its role in navigating the complex emotions and experiences that arise in the face of loss caused by violent crime. By understanding the psychological and emotional benefits of forgiveness, exploring the barriers that hinder its attainment, and offering practical exercises for cultivating forgiveness, we aim to illuminate the transformative potential of forgiveness as a path towards healing and resilience.

15.1.1 The Importance Of Addressing Loss And Trauma

Losing a loved one to a violent crime is an unimaginable tragedy that leaves a lasting impact on the lives of the survivors. The aftermath of such a traumatic event often involves profound grief, anger, and feelings of injustice. While there is no easy way to cope with this devastating loss, one concept that has gained attention in recent years is forgiveness. Forgiveness, in this context, refers to the act of letting go of anger and resentment towards the perpetrator and finding a path towards healing. Understanding the role of forgiveness in coping with loss caused by a violent crime can offer insights into the complexities of grief and provide a potential avenue for healing and personal growth.

15.2 Understanding The Impact Of Violent Crime On Individuals And Communities

15.2.1 The Psychological And Emotional Aftermath Of Violent Crime

The impact of violent crime extends far beyond the immediate physical harm inflicted. Survivors often experience a range of psychological and emotional consequences, including post-traumatic stress disorder (PTSD), depression, anxiety, and survivor's guilt. The traumatic event can shatter one's sense of safety and security, leaving them vulnerable and struggling to come to terms with their new reality. Understanding the psychological and emotional aftermath of violent crime is crucial in recognizing the depth of the pain and trauma experienced by survivors.

15.2.2 Societal Repercussions And Community Trauma

Violent crimes not only affect individuals but also have long-lasting effects on communities. The ripple effect of a single act of violence can be felt far and wide, causing fear, distrust, and a sense of collective trauma within a community. The loss of life and the disruption caused by violent crimes can leave lasting scars on the social fabric, impacting relationships, community cohesion, and even the overall sense of safety. Recognizing the broader societal repercussions of violent crime helps shed light on the collective healing that is necessary beyond individual forgiveness.

15.3 The Complex Nature Of Forgiveness Its Role In Healing

15.3.1 Defining Forgiveness: A Multidimensional Perspective

Forgiveness is a multifaceted concept that involves more than simply pardoning the offender. It is a process that varies from person to person and cannot be forced or rushed. Forgiveness does not imply condoning the actions of the perpetrator but rather acknowledges the survivor's choice to release negative emotions and find their own path to healing. It involves a shift in perspective and a conscious decision to let go of the resentment that may be holding one back from moving forward.

15.3.2 The Connection Between Forgiveness And Personal Growth

Forgiveness has the potential to be a catalyst for personal growth and transformation. By choosing to forgive, survivors can reclaim their power and break free from the grip of anger and resentment. It allows them to redirect their focus from the past towards rebuilding their lives and finding meaning and purpose in the face of tragedy. Forgiveness can open doors to emotional healing, increased resilience, and a renewed sense of hope.

15.4 Psychological And Emotional Benefits Of Forgiveness: An Aid In Coping With Grief And Trauma

15.4.1 Healing The Wounds Of Grief Through Forgiveness

One of the psychological benefits of forgiveness is its potential to facilitate the healing of grief. By forgiving, survivors can release the heavy burden of anger and bitterness that often accompanies the grieving process. It provides an opportunity to honor the memory of their loved one and find solace in the knowledge that holding onto negativity will not bring them back. Forgiveness allows survivors to create space for acceptance, healing, and fostering a connection with their lost loved one in a more positive and constructive manner.

15.4.2 Reducing Anger, Resentment, And Bitterness Through Forgiveness

Anger, resentment, and bitterness are natural responses to the injustice and pain caused by a violent crime. However, holding onto these negative emotions can hinder the healing process and impede personal growth. Forgiveness offers a way to release these toxic emotions, allowing survivors to experience emotional freedom and reclaim control over their lives. By choosing forgiveness, survivors can break free from the cycle of anger and resentment, opening themselves up to the possibility of a more fulfilling and meaningful future.

Understanding the concept of forgiveness in coping with loss caused by a violent crime is not about dismissing the magnitude of the pain or expecting a quick fix. It is about acknowledging the potential healing power that forgiveness holds and recognizing the importance of addressing the complex emotions and trauma associated with such profound loss. While forgiveness may not immediately be the path for everyone, exploring its role in the healing journey can provide insights and options for those navigating the challenging aftermath of a violent crime.

15.5 Challenges To Forgiveness And Strategies To Overcome Them

15.5.1 Addressing Feelings Of Injustice And Seeking Justice

When faced with the loss caused by a violent crime, it is natural to feel a deep sense of injustice. The desire for justice can often be a barrier to forgiveness, as it may seem incompatible with forgiving the perpetrator. It is important to address these feelings of injustice and seek justice in a way that aligns with personal values and beliefs. This may involve working with law enforcement, engaging in legal proceedings, or participating in advocacy efforts for change. By actively pursuing justice, individuals can find a sense of empowerment and closure, which can help facilitate the forgiveness process.

15.5.2 Dealing With The Fear Of Re-Victimization

One of the biggest challenges to forgiveness is the fear of re-victimization. After experiencing a violent crime, it is common to have heightened feelings of vulnerability and a fear of similar incidents occurring again. This fear can make it difficult to let go of resentment and anger towards the offender. To overcome this barrier, it is important to prioritize personal safety and take necessary precautions. Building a strong support network, seeking professional help, and learning self-defense techniques can help individuals regain a sense of security and reduce the fear of re-victimization. By addressing this fear head-on, individuals can free themselves from the shackles of unforgiveness.

15.6 Cultivating Forgiveness: Exploring Practical Techniques And Exercises To Facilitate The Forgiveness Process

15.6.1 Self-Reflection And Self-Compassion As A Foundation For Forgiveness

Self-reflection and self-compassion are essential practices when it comes to cultivating forgiveness. Taking the time to reflect on one's own emotions, thoughts, and experiences can provide valuable insights into the reasons behind resistance to forgiveness. It is important to acknowledge and validate one's own pain and suffering, allowing for self-compassion to emerge. By treating oneself with kindness and understanding, individuals can begin to heal and open up to the possibility of forgiveness.

15.6.2 Mindfulness And Empathy: Tools For Fostering Forgiveness

Mindfulness and empathy are powerful tools in the forgiveness journey. Mindfulness involves being fully present in the moment, non-judgmentally observing thoughts and emotions. By practicing mindfulness, individuals can develop a deeper understanding of their own pain and the pain of others. This understanding can pave the way for empathy, which is the ability to put oneself in another person's shoes and feel their emotions. Cultivating empathy allows individuals to see the humanity in both themselves and the offender, making forgiveness a more attainable goal.

15.7 Forgiveness And Restorative Justice In The Context Of Restorative Justice Approaches

15.7.1 Exploring Restorative Justice Principles And Processes

Restorative justice emphasizes healing and repairing the harm caused by a crime through a collaborative process that involves all stakeholders. While forgiveness is not a requirement in restorative justice, it can play a significant role in promoting healing and reconciliation. Restorative justice practices, such as victim-offender dialogues or mediation, provide opportunities for victims to express their pain and for offenders to take responsibility for their actions. In this context, forgiveness can be seen as a means to restore broken relationships and foster a sense of closure for both parties involved.

15.7.2 The Power Of Forgiveness In Promoting Healing And Reconciliation Within Restorative Justice

Forgiveness has the power to transform relationships within the framework of restorative justice. When victims are able to forgive offenders, it can lead to a sense of liberation and empowerment. Similarly, when offenders sincerely seek forgiveness and express remorse, it can create opportunities for redemption and personal growth. By embracing forgiveness within restorative justice, healing and reconciliation can take place, ultimately contributing to a safer and more compassionate society.

15.8 The Long Journey Of Forgiveness And Its Evolution In The Healing Process

15.8.1 Forgiveness As A Lifelong Process

Forgiveness is not a one-time event but rather a lifelong process. Healing from the loss caused by a violent crime takes time, and forgiveness may come in stages. It is important to be patient with oneself and acknowledge that forgiveness does not mean forgetting or condoning the actions of the offender. Instead, it is about finding inner peace and breaking free from the emotional burdens carried as a result of the crime. Embracing forgiveness as an ongoing journey allows individuals to navigate the complexities of healing and continue to grow and evolve.

15.8.2 The Role Of Support Networks And Therapy In The Forgiveness Process

Support networks and therapy play a crucial role in the forgiveness process. Surrounding oneself with understanding and empathetic individuals can provide a safe space to express emotions and receive validation. Therapeutic interventions, such as counseling or support groups, can offer guidance and tools to navigate the challenges of forgiveness. These resources can provide practical strategies for managing anger, grief, and other emotions, while also offering opportunities for personal growth and development. By engaging with a support network and seeking therapy, individuals can find the strength and resilience needed to embark on the path to forgiveness.

In conclusion, forgiveness is not a simple or linear process, especially when faced with the devastating impact of violent crime. However, by acknowledging the importance of addressing loss and trauma, understanding the profound effects of violence, and embracing forgiveness as a tool for personal growth and healing, individuals and communities can begin to navigate the complex journey of forgiveness. By cultivating self-reflection, empathy, and mindfulness, and by seeking support and exploring restorative justice approaches, we can embark on a path towards healing, reconciliation, and a brighter future. While forgiveness may take time and effort, it holds the potential to bring solace, peace, and a renewed sense of strength in the face of unimaginable loss caused by violent crime.

16. Conclusion: Farewell And Condolences To Those Affected By Violent Crime

Understanding the true nature and complexities of violent crime is of utmost significance for those who find themselves grappling with the overwhelming sorrow and anguish that accompanies the tragic loss of their beloved to these abhorrent acts.

In this book, we have delved deep into the heart-wrenching world of eulogies, seeking to provide solace and guidance to those who have been affected by the devastating consequences of violent crime. By exploring the profound emotions and intricate nuances that surround such a profound loss, we aim to offer a source of comfort and support during this most challenging time.

Through the pages of this book, we have endeavored to shed light on the multifaceted aspects of eulogies, recognizing their power to honor and celebrate the lives of those taken from us too soon. By delving into the art of crafting meaningful tributes, we hope to empower individuals to express their love, admiration, and cherished memories in a way that truly captures the essence of their departed loved ones.

Moreover, we have sought to emphasize the importance of acknowledging the unique circumstances surrounding violent crime. By addressing the complexities and sensitivities inherent in these tragic events, we aim to provide a comprehensive understanding of the challenges faced by those who have suffered such unimaginable loss. Through this understanding, we hope to foster a sense of unity and compassion among those who have experienced similar pain, creating a supportive community that can navigate the path to healing together.

In conclusion, this book serves as a guiding light for those who have been thrust into the darkness of grief by the cruel hand of violent crime. By offering insights, inspiration, and practical advice, we aspire to empower individuals to honor their loved ones with heartfelt eulogies that pay tribute to their lives and provide solace to those left behind. May this book serve as a beacon of hope, reminding us all that even in the face of unimaginable tragedy, love, remembrance and forgiveness can bring solitude, healing and closure.

Frequently Asked Questions
A. Writing The Eulogy

A.1 Can anyone contribute to the eulogy?

Yes, absolutely. The eulogy is an opportunity for friends, family members, and loved ones to share their personal memories and reflections on the deceased's life. If you would like to contribute to the eulogy, reach out to the person organizing the service or the individual designated to speak during the ceremony.

A.2 How long should the eulogy be?

The length of the eulogy can vary depending on the traditions, preferences, and time constraints of the memorial service. Generally, a eulogy is around 5 to 10 minutes long, allowing enough time to capture the essence of the departed's life and impact. However, it is important to remember that quality matters more than quantity. Focus on sharing meaningful stories and heartfelt messages that truly honor your loved one.

A.3 Can I include humor in the eulogy?

Yes, incorporating lighthearted and humorous anecdotes can be a beautiful way to celebrate the joyful moments and unique personality of the departed. However, it is essential to strike a balance and be mindful of the overall tone of the service. Ensure that any humor is respectful and appropriate for the occasion, keeping in mind the feelings of the grieving family and attendees.

A.4 Is it necessary to follow a particular structure for the eulogy?

While there is no one-size-fits-all structure for a eulogy, it is helpful to have a loose outline to guide your speech. Consider including sections such as an introduction, sharing personal memories, highlighting achievements and contributions, discussing the impact on loved ones, and concluding with a heartfelt farewell. However, feel free to adapt the structure to best reflect the unique life and relationships shared with your loved one.

A.5 How can I structure the eulogy for maximum impact?

To ensure the eulogy resonates with the audience, organizing it in a cohesive and impactful manner is key. Begin with an introduction that captures attention and expresses gratitude for the life of our colleague. Then, progress through personal stories, highlighting their achievements, character traits, and moments that made them special. Conclude with a heartfelt message that leaves the listeners feeling uplifted and motivated to honor their memory.

B. About Eulogies For Crime Related Deaths

B.1 Can I include details about the criminal acts in the eulogy?

While it is important to acknowledge the tragic circumstances surrounding the loss, consider the sensitivity of the situation. Focus on honoring the memory of the deceased and celebrating their life rather than dwelling on the specific details of the criminal acts.

B.2 How can I support the grieving community affected by the loss?

Supporting the grieving community is crucial during this difficult time. Offer your presence, lend a listening ear, and provide practical support. Additionally, encourage community resources, such as counseling services or support groups, that can help individuals navigate their grief.

B.3 How can I find strength and resilience in the face of such tragedy?

Grieving the loss of a loved one to criminal acts can be immensely challenging. Seek support from friends, family, or professionals who can help you process your emotions. Engage in self-care practices, such as exercise, therapy, or meditation, and find solace in connecting with others who have experienced similar situations.

B.4 Is it appropriate to mention the criminal justice system or advocate for change in the eulogy?
Deciding whether to mention the criminal justice system or advocate for change in the eulogy is a personal choice. Consider the wishes of the deceased and their family, as well as the tone and context of the gathering. If it aligns with their values and you feel it would be respectful and appropriate, you can address the need for justice or share their desire for positive change.

C. Forgiveness And Coping With Loss

C.1 Can forgiveness truly help in coping with the loss caused by a violent crime?
Forgiveness can play a significant role in the healing process after a violent crime. While it may not erase the pain or undo the past, forgiveness can provide psychological and emotional benefits, such as reducing anger, resentment, and bitterness. It allows individuals to release the heavy burden of negative emotions and find a sense of peace and closure.

C.2 Is forgiveness a one-time event or an ongoing process?
Forgiveness is often a journey rather than a one-time event. It may require time, effort, and self-reflection. The process of forgiveness can evolve and change over time as individuals navigate their grief, trauma, and emotions. It is important to approach forgiveness with patience and compassion, recognizing that it may involve setbacks and moments of reevaluation.

C.3 What are some common barriers to forgiveness after a violent crime?

There are several barriers that can hinder the forgiveness process. Feelings of injustice, the fear of re-victimization, and a desire for justice can make forgiveness challenging. Additionally, societal pressure, cultural beliefs, and the perception that forgiveness means condoning the act of violence can also create obstacles. It is crucial to address these barriers and seek support to navigate the complex emotions and challenges that arise during the forgiveness journey.

C.4 How can restorative justice approaches contribute to the forgiveness process?

Restorative justice approaches can provide a framework for healing and reconciliation after a violent crime. By bringing together victims, offenders, and the community in a facilitated dialogue, restorative justice aims to repair the harm caused and foster understanding. In this context, forgiveness can play a vital role in promoting healing, empathy, and ultimately, the possibility of moving forward with renewed hope and resolution.

D. Finding Closure

D.1 Why is closure important in the aftermath of a crime?

Closure plays a vital role in the healing process for victims' families and friends. It provides a sense of resolution, allowing individuals to come to terms with the loss, grief, and trauma caused by the crime. Closure helps in finding peace, moving forward, and rebuilding lives shattered by the tragic event.

D.2 How can commemorative events contribute to the search for closure?

Commemorative events offer an opportunity to honor the memory of the victim, bring communities together, and provide a space for shared healing. These events, such as memorials, vigils, and dedications, allow people to grieve collectively, find support, and pay tribute to the life that was lost. Such gatherings can contribute significantly to the process of closure.

D.3 Is closure always achievable in cases involving crimes?

Closure may look different for each individual, and it is not always achievable in the same way. Some cases may remain unresolved, leaving certain questions unanswered. However, through various coping strategies, seeking justice, and finding personal ways to remember and honor the victim, a sense of closure can still be attained, even in the absence of complete resolution.

D.4 How can community engagement help in the pursuit of closure?

Community engagement is crucial in supporting victims' families and friends during their journey towards closure. By standing together, advocating for change, and working collaboratively with local organizations and law enforcement, communities can create a safer environment while fostering a sense of unity and empowerment for those affected by the crime.

Other Books/Ebooks In The (Eulogies: From Grieving To Healing Series)

Eulogies When Christmas Becomes A Time Of Loss And Grief: Writing Guidelines, Examples And Templates (ISBN-13: 978-1-960176-17-2)

Eulogies When Accidental Death Takes Our Beloved: Writing Guidelines, Examples and Templates (ISBN-13: 978-1-960176-16-5)

Eulogies When Long-Term Illness Takes Our Beloved: Writing Guidelines, Examples and Templates (ISBN-13: 978-1-960176-15-8)

Eulogies For Those We Lost To Sudden Illness: Writing Guidelines, Examples, and Templates (ISBN-13: 978-1-960176-14-1)